Watermelon

Cookbook

40 New Watermelon Recipes

BY: Nancy Silverman

COPYRIGHT NOTICES

My Heartfelt Thanks and A Special Reward for Your Purchase!

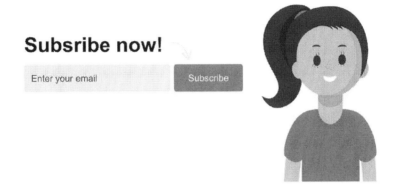

https://nancy.gr8.com

My heartfelt thanks at purchasing my book and I hope you enjoy it! As a special bonus, you will now be eligible to receive books absolutely free on a weekly basis! Get started by entering your email address in the box above to subscribe. A notification will be emailed to you of my free promotions, no purchase necessary! With little effort, you will be eligible for free and discounted books daily. In addition to this amazing gift, a reminder will be sent 1-2 days before the offer expires to remind you not to miss out. Enter now to start enjoying this special offer!

Table of Contents

Drinks

||||||||||||||||||||||||||||||||||||||||||||||||||||||||||||||||||||||

(1) White Wine Watermelon Spritzer

An unoaked Chardonnay works best with this spritzer.

Yield: 6

Preparation Time: 3mins

Total Cooking Time: 3mins

Ingredient List:

- 2 cups seedless watermelon (diced, chilled)
- 1 bottle Chardonnay (chilled)
- 2 tablespoons grenadine syrup
- 12 ounces sparkling mineral water (chilled)

||||||||||||||||||||||||||||||||||||||||||||||||||||||||||||

Instructions:

Divide the watermelon equally between 6 chilled wine glasses. Divide the remaining 3 ingredients between the 6 glasses and stir.

Serve chilled.

(2) Creamy Watermelon Milkshake

Indulgently creamy and refreshing. You would never know these milkshakes are low calorie and vegan-friendly!

Yield: 2

Preparation Time: 5mins

Total Cooking Time: 5mins

Ingredient List:

- 2 cups cubed watermelon (frozen)
- 2 cups almond coconut milk, unsweetened
- 2 teaspoons sweetener

||||||||||||||||||||||||||||||||||||||||||||||||||||||||||||||||||||

Instructions:

Combine all ingredients in a blender and blitz until smooth. Pour equally into two tall glasses and serve.

(3) Watermelon Piña Colada

A fresh new take on everyone's favorite Piña Colada.

Yield: 1

Preparation Time: 2mins

Total Cooking Time: 2mins

Ingredient List:

- 3 ounces pineapple juice
- 2 ounces white rum
- 1 ounce coconut milk
- 3 1" cubes fresh watermelon
- 1 cup ice

||||||||||||||||||||||||||||||||||||||||||||||||||||||||||||

Instructions:

Toss all ingredients in a blender and blitz until smooth.

Serve immediately.

(4) Minted Watermelon Frozen Margaritas

We love this lighter, less sour take on the classic lime Margarita.

Yield: 4-5

Preparation Time: 10mins

Total Cooking Time: 4hours 10mins

Ingredient List:

- 4 cups fresh watermelon (deseeded, chopped)
- Freshly squeezed lime juice
- White sugar
- ½ cup white tequila
- ¼ cup white sugar
- 1 tablespoon lime zest (grated)
- Juice of 3 limes
- 2 tablespoons fresh mint (chopped)

||||||||||||||||||||||||||||||||||||||||||||||||||||||||||||||||

Instructions:

Freeze the watermelon for approximately 4 hours.

Take 4 margarita glasses. Add lime juice and sugar into two separate shallow dishes. Dip each glass rim first in lime juice and then in sugar to coat.

Add all of the remaining ingredients, as well as the frozen watermelon, to a blender and blitz until smooth. Pour evenly into the rimmed glasses and serve!

(5) Watermelon Lemonade

When temperatures soar, sip on this super cooling watermelon lemonade.

Yield: 8-10

Preparation Time: 7mins

Total Cooking Time: 7mins

Ingredient List:

- 6 cups cubed watermelon (deseeded)
- 4 cups very cold water
- ¾ cup freshly squeezed lemon juice (well chilled)
- ⅔ cup white sugar
- Mint (to garnish)

|||||||||||||||||||||||||||||||||||||||||||||||||||||||||||||||

Instructions:

Puree the watermelon in a blender. Strain into a large pitcher.

Add the water, lemon juice, and sugar to the same pitcher. Stir well until the sugar dissolves. Fill with ice and garnish with mint. Serve.

(6) Superfruit Smoothie

Lots of vitamins and minerals in this power packed drink.

Yield: 2

Preparation Time: 2mins

Total Cooking Time: 2mins

Ingredient List:

- 2 cups watermelon (cubed)
- 1 cup frozen raspberries
- 1 cup raspberry kefir
- 2 tablespoons orange juice concentrate
- 2 tablespoons hemp seeds
- 2 tablespoons agave syrup

||||||||||||||||||||||||||||||||||||||||||||||||||||||||||

Instructions:

Put all 6 ingredients into a food blender and blitz until silky.

(7) Watermelon Bellini

The ultimate brunch tipple; sparkling Italian Prosecco fused with sweet watermelon.

Yield: 8

Preparation Time: 10mins

Total Cooking Time: 10mins

Ingredient List:

- Juice of ½ a lime
- 3 cups frozen watermelon (deseeded)
- 1 cup + extra Prosecco (well chilled)
- 2 tablespoons white sugar
- ¼ teaspoon salt

||||||||||||||||||||||||||||||||||||||||||||||||||||||||||||||||||

Instructions:

Add all ingredients to a blender and blitz until smooth. Pour evenly into champagne flutes and top, until full, with a little more Prosecco. Serve!

(8) Tropical Vodka Watermelon Cooler

This refreshing tipple is packed with fresh fruity flavor.

Yield: 4

Preparation Time: 10mins

Total Cooking Time: 10mins

Ingredient List:

- 10 ounces frozen strawberries in syrup
- 1 cup ice
- 1 cup fresh watermelon (cubed)
- ½ cup vodka
- ½ cup pineapple juice
- ¼ cup cream of coconut

||||||||||||||||||||||||||||||||||||||||||||||||||||||||||||

Instructions:

Add the strawberries to a blender and blitz until you have a smooth puree. Pour the puree evenly into four glasses.

Add the remaining ingredients to the blender and blitz again until smooth. Pour the vodka mixture over the purée in the glasses. Serve immediately!

(9) Watermelon and Coconut Milk

A creamy, indulgent drink for any time of the day or night, any month of the year.

Yield: 2

Preparation Time: 2mins

Total Cooking Time: 2mins

Ingredient List:

- 2 cups watermelon chunks
- ⅓ cup light coconut milk
- 2 tablespoons coconut flakes
- ¼ teaspoon vanilla extract
- 4 ice cubes

|||||||||||||||||||||||||||||||||||||||||||||||||||||||||||||

Instructions:

Place all 5 ingredients in a food blender and blitz until silky.

Serve chilled.

(10) Watermelon and Coconut Ball Cocktail

Your guests will love this creamy cocktail.

Yield: 4

Preparation Time: 3mins

Total Cooking Time: 3mins

Ingredient List:

- 6 ounces chilled watermelon purée
- 4 scoops watermelon (chilled)
- 1 cup shredded coconut
- 3 ounces chilled crème de cacao

||||||||||||||||||||||||||||||||||||||||||||||||||||||||||||||||

Instructions:

To make the watermelon purée, remove seeds from the watermelon and slice into large sized chunks. Place in a blender and blitz until silky.

Using a melon scoop, make 4 small watermelon balls. Dredge the watermelon in the shredded coconut.

In martini glasses, mix the watermelon puree with the crème de cacao. Place the coconut shredded watermelon ball in the middle of each glass and serve.

Appetizers

||||||||||||||||||||||||||||||||||||||||||||||||||||||||||||||||||||

(1) Watermelon, Pecan, and Red Pepper Jelly Salad

The winning ingredient in this mouthwatering salad is the addition of homemade vinaigrette.

Yield: 6-8

Preparation Time: 20mins

Total Cooking Time: 40mins

Ingredient List:

Vinaigrette

- ⅓ cup red wine vinegar
- ¼ cup olive oil
- 3 tablespoons store bought red pepper jelly
- 1 small shallot (minced)
- 1 teaspoon stone ground mustard
- ¼ teaspoon salt
- ¼ teaspoon fresh ground black pepper

Salad

- ¾ cup chopped pecans
- 5 cups watermelon (seeded, cubed)
- 1 (6 ounce) package mâche (washed)
- 1 cup Gorgonzola cheese (crumbled)

Instructions:

Preheat the main oven to 350 degrees F.

To make the pepper jelly dressing: Place all 7 ingredients in a mixing bowl and whisk to combine. Set the dressing aside.

Scatter the pecans in a single layer on a baking tray or sheet, and cook in the preheated oven for 5-7 minutes, until lightly toasted. When cooked cool on a rack for around 15 minutes or until cool.

In a large bowl combine the watermelon and mache (lamb's lettuce), add the pepper jelly vinaigrette and toss to coat. Transfer the watermelon mixture to a large serving platter, and sprinkle with the cooked pecans and Gorgonzola cheese.

(2) Blue Cheese and Prosciutto Grilled Watermelon

Sweet watermelon is the perfect partner to salty blue cheese and prosciutto

Yield: 4

Preparation Time: 5mins

Total Cooking Time: 20mins

Ingredient List:

- 12 watermelon wedges (½" thick)
- 1 tablespoon olive oil
- Black pepper and sea salt (to taste)
- 4 ounces prosciutto (thinly sliced)
- 4 ounces fresh blue cheese (crumbled)
- Small handful fresh basil
- 2 teaspoons balsamic glaze

IIIIIIIIIIIIIIIIIIIIIIIIIIIIIIIIIIIIIIIIIIIIIIIIIIIIIIIIIII

Instructions:

Preheat grill to 375 degrees F.

Brush each piece of watermelon with a little oil and season with black pepper and sea salt.

Grill the watermelon for a minute on each side, until grill marks appear.

Arrange the grilled melon on a serving platter. Arrange the prosciutto on top and crumble over the blue cheese. Scatter the basil over the top and finish with a drizzle of balsamic. Serve.

(3) Watermelon Bruschetta with Feta and Balsamic

Sweet and savory. A perfect light bite for the summer.

Yield: 8

Preparation Time: 15mins

Total Cooking Time: 35mins

Ingredient List:

- 1 baguette (cut into 1 ½" thick slices)
- 1 cup balsamic vinegar
- 2 tablespoons honey
- 1 cup Feta cheese crumbles
- ¼ cup part skim ricotta cheese
- 2½ cups fresh seedless watermelon (finely chopped)
- 3 tablespoons fresh basil (chopped)
- 2 tablespoons fresh chives (chopped)
- Freshly cracked black pepper

|||||||||||||||||||||||||||||||||||||||||||||||||||||||||||||||||

Instructions:

Lay the slices of baguette on a baking tray or sheet and grill for 2-3 minutes, or until golden brown and crispy.

In a medium saucepan, on a medium-high heat, combine the vinegar, along with the honey, and heat. Stir constantly, while allowing the mixture to reach a simmer. Once simmering has been achieved, reduce the heat a little in order to keep at simmering point. Stir once or twice, and remove the pan from the heat as soon as the mixture has thickened and reduced by half. This should take around 15-20 minutes.

Combine the crumbled Feta and ricotta cheese in a food blender or processor and blitz until smooth. You may add extra cheese of either/both variety in order to reach your preferred level of consistency.

Spread the whipped feta on top of the toasted slices. Top with the chopped watermelon. Season with pepper, basil, and chives. Drizzle with the balsamic reduction.

(4) Chilled Watermelon Soup

A refreshing alternative to Spanish Gazpacho soup.

Yield: 2-4

Preparation Time: 5mins

Total Cooking Time: 8hours 5mins

Ingredient List:

- 7 pounds watermelon flesh (no seeds)
- ½ cup plain Greek yogurt
- 1 teaspoon fresh ginger (grated)
- Juice of ½ lemon
- Pinch sea salt
- Dash ground nutmeg
- 6 mint leaves (chopped)
- Handful walnuts (crushed)

||||||||||||||||||||||||||||||||||||||||||||||||||||||||||||||

Instructions:

Add the watermelon, yogurt, ginger, lemon juice, salt, nutmeg and mint leaves to a food blender and blitz until totally combined.

Transfer to the refrigerator to chill, preferably overnight.

Garnish with crushed walnuts.

(5) Watermelon and Feta Salad

A light lunch or snack. The sweetness of the fruit complements the feta flavors perfectly.

Yield: 4

Preparation Time: 10mins

Total Cooking Time: 10mins

Ingredient List:

- 2 cups watermelon (cubed)
- 2 cups strawberries (hulled, chopped)
- ½ cup Feta (crumbled)
- ¼ cup virgin olive oil
- Sea salt
- Black pepper
- ¼ cup fresh basil (torn)

||||||||||||||||||||||||||||||||||||||||||||||||||||||||||||||

Instructions:

In a large salad bowl, using wooden utensils, combine the watermelon, strawberries, Feta, and oil. Season well with sea salt and pepper. Toss thoroughly to coat.

Garnish with torn basil and serve.

(6) Crab Cakes and Watermelon Chili Relish

A flavorsome appetizer to serve at a dinner party. You could also increase the amounts and serve as party finger food.

Yield: 8

Preparation Time: 5mins

Total Cooking Time: 15mins

Ingredients;

- 8 ounces cooked crabmeat (shelled, drained)
- 2 eggs (lightly beaten)
- 1 tablespoon mayonnaise
- ½ cup seasoned breadcrumbs
- ¼ cup sweet pickle relish (drained)
- 3 tablespoons butter for frying
- 1 cup watermelon (minced, drained)
- ½ cup bottled chili sauce

||||||||||||||||||||||||||||||||||||||||||||||||||||||||||||||||

Instructions:

In a large mixing bowl combine the crabmeat, beaten eggs, mayonnaise, seasoned breadcrumbs and pickle relish.

In a 12" frying pan over medium-high heat, melt the butter. Drop 1 heaping teaspoonful of the crab mixture into the melted butter and sauté. Flatten to form a cake and turn once, until golden brown all over. Repeat the process until all the crab mixture has been used. Sauté in batches, keeping the crab cakes warm on a baking tray in a warmed oven.

Combine the watermelon and chili sauce, and serve as a dipping sauce on a bed of lettuce.

(7) Spicy Summer Guacamole

Sweet watermelon helps to cool the fiery habanero chilies in this addictive guacamole. Serve with tortilla chips for a great sharing appetizer.

Yield: 8

Preparation Time: 5mins

Total Cooking Time: 20mins

Ingredient List:

- 4 ripe avocados (peeled, pitted)
- ⅛ cup green onions (minced)
- 1 ripe tomato (deseeded, finely diced)
- 2 habanero chilies (deseeded, minced)
- ¼ cup watermelon (finely diced)
- 1 tablespoon freshly squeezed lemon juice
- ¼ teaspoon sea salt
- Tortilla chips (for serving)

|||||||||||||||||||||||||||||||||||||||||||||||||||||||||||||

Instructions:

Add the avocado to a bowl and mash with a fork. Add in the remaining ingredients and stir gently until totally combined. Allow to stand for 10-15 minutes to allow flavors to intensify. Serve with tortilla chips!

(8) Fresh Creamy Shrimp Salad with Watermelon

Creamy shrimp salad sits on top a slice of fresh seasoned watermelon.

Yield: 4

Preparation Time: 10mins

Total Cooking Time: 12mins

Ingredient List:

- 4 slices rindless watermelon (1" thick)
- Sea salt and black pepper (to taste)
- 1 tablespoon sweet onion (finely chopped)
- 3 tablespoons full-fat mayo
- 2 tablespoons celery (finely chopped)
- 1 tablespoon lemon zest
- 3 tablespoons freshly squeezed lemon juice
- 1-pound cooked shrimp (peeled)
- 2 tablespoons fresh tarragon (chopped)
- 5 ounces baby arugula

Instructions:

Arrange the watermelon on a serving plate. Season with salt and pepper.

Add the sweet onion to a bowl and cook in the microwave for 30 seconds. Remove and add in the mayo, chopped celery, lemon zest, one tablespoon of lemon juice, shrimp and tarragon. Stir gently until totally combined. Season with more salt and pepper.

In a medium bowl, add the arugula and sprinkle over the remaining lemon zest and juice. Toss to combine and season. Arrange the arugula on top of the watermelon and then spoon the shrimp salad over the top. Serve.

(9) Scallop Watermelon Ceviche

Ceviche is a dish that uses citrus juice to 'cook' the seafood, resulting in a zesty fresh dish bursting with flavor.

Yield: 5-6

Preparation Time: 7mins

Total Cooking Time: 2hours 10mins

Ingredient List:

- 1 cup pureed watermelon
- ½ cup freshly squeezed lime juice
- 1 tablespoon freshly squeezed lemon juice
- 1 tablespoon good quality vodka
- ⅛ cup fresh parsley (minced)
- 1 tablespoon fresh chives (minced)
- ¼ teaspoon sea salt
- ¼ teaspoon pepper
- 1-pound fresh scallops (sushi grade)

||||||||||||||||||||||||||||||||||||||||||||||||||||||||||||||

Instructions:

In a bowl, combine all ingredients (excluding the scallops) and stir well until combined.

Take the scallops and slice them a ¼" thick. Drop the sliced scallops into the sauce and stir gently.

Refrigerate for 2 hours, covered. Allow to sit at room temperature for 3-4 minutes before serving!

(10) Meatballs in Watermelon Glaze

A delicious appetizer – perfect, served on a bed of crisp lettuce.

Yield: 8

Preparation Time: 4mins

Total Cooking Time: 12mins

Ingredient List:

- 2 tablespoons vegetable oil
- 36 frozen ready-made mini meatballs
- 1 cup BBQ (store bought)
- 1 cup pureed watermelon

|||||||||||||||||||||||||||||||||||||||||||||||||||||||||||||||

Instructions:

In a large frying pan heat the vegetable oil over high heat. Sauté the meatballs until browned all over and hot in the center. Reduce the heat to a low setting.

In a small bowl combine the barbecue sauce along with the watermelon puree. Pour the puree over the mini meatballs and simmer for 2-3 minutes. Serve piping hot.

Mains

||||||||||||||||||||||||||||||||||||||||||||||||||||||||||||||||||

(1) Watermelon Pad Thai

Watermelon gives Pad Thai a melon makeover; a refreshing twist to a traditional dish.

Yield: 4

Preparation Time: 5mins

Total Cooking Time: 25mins

Ingredient List:

- 8 ounces rice noodles
- Boiling water
- ¼ cup canola oil
- 1 tablespoon fresh garlic (minced)
- 1 tablespoon ginger (minced)
- 1-pound medium shrimp (cleaned)
- 1 teaspoon soy sauce
- 1 cup bean sprouts
- ½ cup fresh cilantro
- ½ cup scallions (chopped)
- ⅛ cup catsup
- 1 cup pureed watermelon
- 1 cup dry roasted peanuts (chopped)

||||||||||||||||||||||||||||||||||||||||||||||||||||||||||||||||||||

Instructions:

Add the rice noodles to a bowl and pour over boiling water. Set to one side to stand for around 10-15 minutes, nudging them with a chopstick so that they don't stick together.

Once the noodles are tender, drain them.

In a large wok heat the oil over med.-high heat. Sauté the minced garlic and ginger for 1 minute and add in the shrimp. Continue to fry for 2-3 minutes while adding the soy sauce.

Add the noodles to the pan and fry for a further couple of minutes. Stir in the bean sprouts, cilantro, and chopped scallions.

Combine the catsup with the pureed watermelon and add to the pan along with the sesame oil.

Cook until heated through, scatter with peanuts and enjoy.

(2) Grilled Duck with Watermelon Glaze

Wow your dinner guests with butterflied duck served with a spicy chile watermelon glaze.

Yield: 4

Preparation Time: 15mins

Total Cooking Time: 2hours 55mins

Ingredient List:

- 2 whole (4 pound) ducks (un-treated)
- Olive oil
- 1 teaspoon sea salt
- ½ teaspoon pepper

Glaze

- ½ small watermelon (flesh only, cut into chunks)
- 1 (12 ounce) jar apple jelly
- 2 teaspoons red chile flakes
- 1 teaspoon jalapeno hot sauce
- Juice and zest of 1 small lime
- Pinch salt

|||||||||||||||||||||||||||||||||||||||||||||||||||||||||||||||||

Instructions:

Preheat the grill on a medium high heat for indirect cooking.

Using kitchen paper, pat the duck dry before cutting along the sides of the duck's backbones, using kitchen shears to remove them. Lay the birds, breast side facing up, and open both sides like a book, flat on a cutting board.

Break the breast bones by applying firm pressure and pressing down. Tuck the tips of the wings under the upper wings and lay on a baking tray or sheet. Brush the ducks all over with oil and season lightly on each side with salt and pepper. Place the duck's skin side facing up in the center of the grill, for around 2 hours.

To make the Spicy Watermelon Glaze: Using a juicer, extract the watermelon juice and set to one side.

In a small saucepan on a low heat, melt the jelly, stirring to prevent it burning. Once the jelly has melted, add the watermelon juice and stir to combine. Next, add the lime juice and lime zest. Add the chile flakes, jalapeno hot sauce, and salt. Season to taste.

Brush the ducks with watermelon glaze, and continue to grill until the juices run totally clear, this should take around 20-30 minutes. Brush with the glaze a couple of times during the cooking process.

Remove the ducks from the grill and brush liberally with the glaze one more time. Set to one side for 8-10 minutes before cutting the duck into quarters. Serve.

(3) Watermelon Beef Stir Fry

Stir fry is a quick and healthy way to feed your family.

Yield: 4-6

Preparation Time: 5mins

Total Cooking Time: 25mins

Ingredient List:

- 1-pound sirloin steak (sliced into strips)
- 2 teaspoons water
- 3 cloves garlic (minced)
- 2 teaspoons cornstarch
- 2 teaspoons low sodium soy sauce
- 1½ teaspoon sesame oil
- 2 tablespoons white wine (divided)
- 2 tablespoons warm water
- 2 tablespoons hoisin sauce
- 2 tablespoons canola oil
- 1 teaspoon sea salt
- ½ teaspoon pepper
- 1 sweet onion (sliced)
- 12 ounces' sugar snap peas
- 1 teaspoon fresh ginger (grated)
- ½ teaspoon red peppercorns (crushed)
- 2 cups fresh watermelon (julienned)
- 2 cups cooked rice (hot)

Instructions:

Add the steak, water, garlic, cornstarch, soy sauce, sesame oil and half of the wine to a bowl. Set aside to marinate for half an hour.

In a small bowl, stir together the warm water, hoisin sauce and remaining wine.

Heat 1½ tablespoons of canola oil in a large wok. Add in the steak (discarding the marinade) and season with salt and pepper. Heat for 2-3 minutes. Add the onion, peas, ginger and red peppercorns. Fry for 2-3 minutes. Pour in the reserved hoisin mixture. Take off the heat and toss in the watermelon.

Season with a little more salt and pepper and serve straight away with rice.

(4) Grilled Grouper Fillets with Watermelon Salsa

Grouper has a mild and slightly sweet flavor which pairs perfectly with this spicy watermelon salsa.

Yield: 4

Preparation Time: 10mins

Total Cooking Time: 18mins

Ingredient List:

- 4 (4 ounce) grouper fillets
- 1 teaspoon freshly ground pepper
- 1 teaspoon salt (divided)
- 3 tablespoons olive oil (divided)
- 2 cups seedless watermelon (chopped)
- ¼ cup kalamata olives (pitted, chopped)
- ½ English cucumber, chopped
- 1 small jalapeño pepper (seeded, minced)
- 2 tablespoons red onion (minced)
- 2 tablespoons white balsamic vinegar

||||||||||||||||||||||||||||||||||||||||||||||||||||||||||||||

Instructions:

Preheat the grill to medium-high heat. Sprinkle the grouper fillets with ground pepper and ½ teaspoon of salt. Drizzle with 2 tablespoonss of olive oil.

Grill the grouper with the lid closed for 3-4 minutes each side, the fish is ready when it flakes easily. The center of the fish should be opaque.

In a medium bowl combine the watermelon, olives, cucumber, pepper, red onion and balsamic vinegar. Add the remaining ½ teaspoon of salt and 1 tablespoon of olive oil.

Serve the watermelon salsa on the side.

(5) Roasted Watermelon Steaks with Cotija Cheese

Roasting peaches and pineapples is quite commonplace – so why not watermelon?

Yield: 2

Preparation Time: 10mins

Total Cooking Time: 2hours 40mins

Ingredient List:

- Cooking spray
- 4 watermelon steaks
- ½ cup cream sherry
- 4 tablespoons unsalted butter
- Salt and pepper to taste
- Vegetable oil
- ¼ cup balsamic vinegar
- Cotija cheese

Instructions:

Preheat the main oven to 350 degrees F. Line a roasting pan with parchment paper lightly misted with cooking spray.

First, prepare the watermelon. Remove the rind and seeds and cut into rectangular slices of approximately 3x4x1½ inches.

Lay the melon slices in the roasting pan. Pour the cream sherry over each slice and dot each slice with butter. Season with salt and pepper. Cover the watermelon with a large piece of parchment paper. Then, using aluminum foil, tightly cover the whole roasting pan.

Transfer to the preheated oven and using a little vegetable oil, roast for 2-2½ hours or until the melon is charred around the edges.

Meanwhile, in a small saucepan, bring the balsamic vinegar to a boil, and reduce the vinegar by half.

When the watermelon is sufficiently roasted, remove it from the oven and serve with cotija cheese. Drizzle with the balsamic vinegar reduction just before serving.

(6) Haddock and Chips with Homemade Watermelon Dipping Sauce

Watermelon makes a perfect dipping sauce when served alongside sweet potato fries. The flavors balance perfectly.

Yield: 4-6

Preparation Time: 10mins

Total Cooking Time: 30mins

Ingredient List:

Dipping sauce

- 2 cups watermelon puree
- ½ cup balsamic vinegar
- ½ cup raw sugar

Fish

- 8 haddock fillets
- 1 cup plain flour
- 1 teaspoon sea salt
- 1 teaspoon black pepper
- 4 medium eggs (beaten)
- 2 cups panko breadcrumbs
- 2 medium-large sweet potatoes
- Parmesan cheese (grated)

Instructions:

In a stainless steel saucepan combine the pureed watermelon, balsamic vinegar, and raw sugar. Bring to a gentle simmer while constantly stirring.

Slowly boil until the mixture reduces by half, and set to one side.

Rinse the haddock and use kitchen paper to pat it dry.

In a medium bowl, mix the flour with the sea salt and black pepper. Sprinkle over both sides of the fish.

Dip each fillet into the egg and then the breadcrumbs.

Very thinly slice the sweet potatoes. Deep fry the coated haddock and potato slices in vegetable oil at 375 degrees F, until the fish flakes easily and the potato chips are crisp.

Drain the fish and chips, scatter with grated Parmesan cheese. Serve the watermelon vinegar reduction on the side as a dip.

(7) Pulled Pork and Watermelon BBQ Sauce

A brand-new take on an old-time favorite. The ultimate cookout family meal.

Yield: 8-12

Preparation Time: 10mins

Total Cooking Time: 5hours 10mins

Ingredient List:

- 5 pounds pork shoulder
- 24 ounces dark beer
- 2 cups BBQ sauce
- 2 cups seedless watermelon (minced)

||||||||||||||||||||||||||||||||||||||||||||||||||||||||||

Instructions:

Slow cook the pork in the dark beer until the meat is so tender that it easily pulls apart.

Cool and trim the pork, discarding any fat. Chop and reheat.

Warm the barbecue sauce and just before you are ready to serve, add the watermelon and stir.

(8) Halibut with Watermelon and Tzatziki

Low in fat and calories, but lots of flavor and taste.

Yield: 4

Preparation Time: 10mins

Total Cooking Time: 20mins

Ingredient List:

- 1 cup watermelon (diced)

Tzatziki

- ¼ cup nonfat, plain Greek yogurt
- ¼ cup cucumber (diced)
- ¼ cup watermelon white rind (diced very small, green skin removed)
- ½ cup fresh mint leaves
- ½ cup cilantro leaves
- 1 tablespoon freshly squeezed lemon juice
- 1 teaspoon lemon zest
- 2 teaspoons white sugar
- 2½ teaspoon minced ginger
- 4 ounces canned diced chilies (drained)
- ¼ teaspoon salt

Halibut

- 4 thick fillets halibut
- Olive oil cooking spray
- Sea salt and pepper (to taste)

||||||||||||||||||||||||||||||||||||||||||||||||||||||||||||||||

Instructions:

First heat the grill.

Lay the diced watermelon on kitchen paper in order to absorb any excess juice. Set the melon to one side.

In a medium sized bowl combine the yogurt, diced cucumber, diced rind, fresh mint, cilantro leaves, lemon juice and zest, white sugar, minced ginger, and chilies. Season with sea salt and pepper to taste. Set aside.

Spray the halibut with cooking spray and season with salt and pepper. Grill for approximately 3-5 minutes, flip over and grill for another 3-5 minutes.

Top each halibut fillet with tzatziki, and scatter over watermelon.

(9) Pork and Watermelon Kebabs

A bright, colorful, healthy meal. Serve with brown rice or a crisp salad.

Yield: 8

Preparation Time: 10mins

Total Cooking Time: 1hour 30mins

Ingredient List:

- 6 tablespoon light brown sugar
- 6 tablespoon soy sauce
- 6 tablespoons red onion (diced)
- 3 cloves garlic (minced)
- 1 tablespoon olive oil
- 3 tablespoons lemon juice
- ¼ teaspoon dried thyme
- ¼ teaspoon pepper
- 1-pound lean pork chop, cut into 40 (1") cubes
- 32 cubes (1") fresh watermelon (deseeded)
- 16 rounds (¾") zucchini
- 16 cubes (1") fresh pineapple
- 24 chunks (1") yellow/orange bell pepper
- Low cal cooking spray

||||||||||||||||||||||||||||||||||||||||||||||||||||||||||||||||

Instructions:

In a large bowl combine the brown sugar, soy sauce, red onion, garlic, olive oil, lemon juice, thyme, and pepper. Pour the ingredients into a zipped bag and add the cubes of pork. Zip the bag, and massage to mix, ensuring all the meat is coated. Transfer the bag to the refrigerator for at least 1 hour, turn the bag a few times.

Remove the pork from the zipped bag, setting the marinade to one side. Thread 5 pieces of pork, 4 cubes of watermelon, 3 rounds of zucchini, 2 chunks of pineapple and 3 peppers on each of the 8 skewers, alternate the order.

Preheat grill to med-high heat. Mist the surface on which you are going to cook with cooking spray. Place the kebabs on the grill. Grill the kebabs for approximately 12-15 minutes, until cooked. Baste and turn frequently with the marinade set aside earlier.

Serve!

(10) Jamaican Jerk Lobster Tacos

Indulgent lobster served with avocado, papaya and watermelon.

Yield: 4-6

Preparation Time: 10mins

Total Cooking Time: 1hour 10mins

Ingredient List:

- 4 rock lobster tails (cooked)
- 2 fresh avocados (peeled, cut into ½" cubes)
- 2 papayas (cut into ½" cubes)
- 2 cups cubed (½") watermelon
- ½ cup fresh cilantro (chopped)
- ½ cup freshly squeezed lime juice
- 2 tablespoons honey
- 1 tablespoon jerk seasoning
- Dash salt and pepper to taste
- 4-6 soft taco shells
- 1 head iceberg lettuce (shredded)
- 1 ounce coconut flakes

IIIIIIIIIIIIIIIIIIIIIIIIIIIIIIIIIIIIIIIIIIIIIIIIIIIIIIIIIIIIIIIIIII

Instructions:

Cut the lobster tails in half lengthwise. Remove the veins and cut into ½" slices. In a large bowl combine the lobster with the cubed watermelon, avocado, papaya, and cilantro.

In a small bowl combine the lime juice with the honey, and jerk seasoning. Season with salt and pepper. Whisk. Pour the honey mixture over the lobster mixture and place in the refrigerator for 1 hour, occasionally stirring.

Place in soft taco shells on top of shredded lettuce and sprinkle generously with shredded coconut.

Desserts

||||||||||||||||||||||||||||||||||||||||||||||||||||||||||||||||||||

(1) Watermelon Yogurt Pops

A healthier sweet treat that your little ones will love.

Yield: 6

Preparation Time: 3mins

Total Cooking Time: 8hours 3mins

Ingredient List:

- 3 cups fresh watermelon (cubed)
- ½ cup full-fat Greek yogurt
- ¼ cup white sugar
- 1 tablespoon freshly squeezed lemon juice
- 6 popsicle sticks

||||||||||||||||||||||||||||||||||||||||||||||||||||||||||||||

Instructions:

Combine all ingredients in a blender and blitz until smooth. Pour equally into a 6 hole popsicle mold. Insert a popsicle stick into each hold.

Freeze overnight.

(2) Cheesecake with Watermelon Topping

A no-bake cheesecake topped with a fresh watermelon, mint and lime topping.

Yield: 8

Preparation Time: 15mins

Total Cooking Time: 3hours 15mins

Ingredient List:

- 1 cup granulated sugar
- 2 cups cream cheese (softened)
- 2 tablespoons watermelon juice
- 2 tablespoons watermelon syrup
- 1 drop red food coloring
- 1 cup heavy cream
- 1 ½ cups cracker crumbs
- ¼ cup brown sugar
- ½ cup butter (melted)

Topping

- 2 cups watermelon (diced)
- 1 tablespoon mint (chopped)
- 3 tablespoons lime juice
- 1 teaspoon watermelon flavoring
- 1 tablespoon sugar

Instructions:

Using an electric mixer, cream the sugar along with the cream cheese until silky. Add the watermelon juice, syrup and food coloring, put to one side.

Whip the heavy cream until it forms stiff peaks. Gently fold the cream into the cream cheese mixture. Use the remaining ingredients to make a crust. Press the crust into a pan, preferably springform. Fill the pan with the cheesecake mixture and transfer to the freezer for 2-3 hours.

Decorate with the freshly made topping.

To make the topping: Combine all the ingredients in a bowl. Mix well and chill in the refrigerator until needed.

(3) Watermelon Sorbet

A fantastic palate cleanser for in between courses or cooling sorbet for that hot summer's day.

Yield: 8

Preparation Time: 5mins

Total Cooking Time: 5hours 5mins

Ingredient List:

- 3 cups frozen watermelon
- 1 tablespoon sugar

||||||||||||||||||||||||||||||||||||||||||||||||||||||||||||||||

Instructions:

In a food blender, blitz the 2 ingredients until totally combined, between 4-5 minutes.

Transfer the mixture to a 9" square loaf pan and freeze until totally solid, this should take around 4-5 hours.

(4) Mini Melon Bites

A great healthy and colorful snack; ideal for a kid's party.

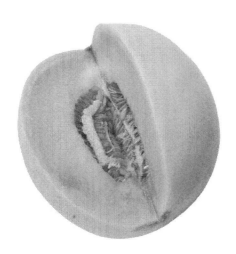 

Yield: 6

Preparation Time: 10mins

Total Cooking Time: 10mins

Ingredient List:

- 1 small watermelon
- 2 cups cool whip
- Rainbow sprinkles

||||||||||||||||||||||||||||||||||||||||||||||||||||||||||||||||

Instructions:

Take a sharp knife and slice off a small portion of the watermelon skin. Stand the melon on the flat edge of a cutting board.

Slice the watermelon into slices of no more than 2" thick.

Take a biscuit cutter (3") and cut small round out of the watermelon slices.

Spoon a dollop of whip onto each watermelon round and scatter with rainbow sprinkles.

(5) Watermelon Ice Cream

The good news is, you don't need an ice cream maker to create this refreshing dessert.

Yield: 6

Preparation Time: 5mins

Total Cooking Time: 5hours 5mins

Ingredient List:

- 2 cups watermelon (cubed)
- 2 cups whole milk
- 2 tablespoons sugar
- ¼ teaspoon vanilla

||||||||||||||||||||||||||||||||||||||||||||||||||||||||||||||

Instructions:

Put all 4 ingredients in a food blender and process until silky. Pour the mixture into a loaf pan and transfer to the freezer for 3 hours.

When the 3 hours have elapsed, remove the ice cream from the pan and then blend again. When processed return the mixture to the pan and freeze it for another 1-2 hours.

Serve.

(6) Raspberry and Pistachio Watermelon Sundae

A sophisticated sundae made with raspberry sorbet and candied pistachios. Serve at your next summer dinner party to cool your guests right down.

Yield: 6

Preparation Time: 5mins

Total Cooking Time: 23mins

Ingredient List:

- 1 egg white (beaten)
- 2 tablespoons maple syrup
- 2 teaspoons light brown sugar
- ¼ teaspoon sea salt
- 1 cup pistachios
- 2 cups watermelon (diced)
- Raspberry sorbet
- 1 cup marshmallow crème (slightly warmed)

||||||||||||||||||||||||||||||||||||||||||||||||||||||||||||

Instructions:

Preheat the main oven to 300 degrees F.

Combine the egg white, maple syrup, brown sugar and salt in a bowl. Add in the pistachios, and toss to combine. Tip out onto a baking sheet and place in the oven for 17-18 minutes. Allow to cool and then break into small pieces.

Add a ⅓ cup watermelon into the base of 5 sundae glasses. Top with a scoop of raspberry sorbet. Drizzle with a little marshmallow crème and finish with a scattering of pistachios. Serve!

(7) Watermelon Blueberry Pancake Stack

Serve this as a weekend breakfast treat or a fun dessert. Your little ones will love them!

Yield: 6

Preparation Time: 5mins

Total Cooking Time: 5mins

Ingredient List:

- 12 (3") blueberry pancakes (cooled)
- ½ cup white vanilla frosting
- 6 (3") discs of watermelon (patted dry with kitchen paper)

||||||||||||||||||||||||||||||||||||||||||||||||||||||||||||||

Instructions:

Take a cooled pancake and spread a generous layer of white vanilla frosting on one side. Place a disc of watermelon on top of the frosted side. Take another pancake and again frost only one side. Place it frosting side down on top of the watermelon to make a watermelon sandwich/stack. Repeat to make another 5 stacks. Enjoy!

(8) Shortbread Cookie Watermelon Crumble

A quick and easy dessert that's a healthier alternative to butter and calorie-laden baked crumbles.

Yield: 8-10

Preparation Time: 5mins

Total Cooking Time: 5mins

Ingredient List:

- 4 shortbread cookies (crumbled)
- 4 cups watermelon (cut into small cubes)
- Sweetened whipped cream

||||||||||||||||||||||||||||||||||||||||||||||||||||||||||||||||

Instructions:

Take a 9x13" pie dish and press half of the cookies into the base. Add the watermelon on top. Sprinkle over the remaining cookies and top with a few dollops of whipped cream. Serve!

(9) Toasted Almond and Cookie Mess

A beautiful mess of toasted slivered almonds, chocolate chip cookies, and fresh watermelon. Serve with a dollop of whip cream.

Yield: 6

Preparation Time: 5mins

Total Cooking Time: 15mins

Ingredient List:

- 1 tbsp salted butter
- 1 cup slivered almonds
- 10 choc chip cookies (crunchy, crumbled)
- 3 cups watermelon (diced)
- 2 cups whipped cream

||||||||||||||||||||||||||||||||||||||||||||||||||||||||||||

Instructions:

Melt the butter in a sauté pan. Add the almonds and cook until they turn golden and the butter begins to foam. Take off the heat and transfer to a plate.

Divide the choc chip cookie crumbles and watermelon evenly onto 6 plates.

Top each with a dollop of whipped cream and then sprinkle over the toasted almonds.

Enjoy.

(10) Sweet Honey and Soy Watermelon Balls

A healthier sweet treat that your little ones will love.

Yield: 2

Preparation Time: 10mins

Total Cooking Time: 10mins

Ingredient List:

- 12 (1½") watermelon balls
- 2 bamboo skewers
- 1 cup powdered sugar
- 1½ cups white sugar
- ¾ cup oyster sauce
- ⅓ cup sherry
- ⅓ cup warm water

||||||||||||||||||||||||||||||||||||||||||||||||||||||||||||||||

Instructions:

Thread 6 watermelon balls onto each bamboo skewer.

Add the powdered sugar to a shallow dish. Roll the watermelon skewers in the sugar and arrange on a plate.

In a small bowl, combine the sugar, oyster sauce, sherry, and water. Stir well until the sugar has dissolved. Pour the sauce over the skewers.

About the Author

Nancy Silverman is an accomplished chef from Essex, Vermont. Armed with her degree in Nutrition and Food Sciences from the University of Vermont, Nancy has excelled at creating e-books that contain healthy and delicious meals that anyone can make and everyone can enjoy. She improved her cooking skills at the New England Culinary Institute in Montpelier Vermont and she has been working at perfecting her culinary style since graduation. She claims that her life's work is always a work in progress and she only hopes to be an inspiration to aspiring chefs everywhere.

Her greatest joy is cooking in her modern kitchen with her family and creating inspiring and delicious meals. She often says that she has perfected her signature dishes based on her family's critique of each and every one.

Nancy has her own catering company and has also been fortunate enough to be head chef at some of Vermont's most exclusive restaurants. When a friend suggested she share some of her outstanding signature dishes, she decided to add cookbook author to her repertoire of personal achievements. Being a technological savvy woman, she felt the e-book realm would be a better fit and soon she had her first cookbook available online. As of today, Nancy has sold over 1,000 e-books and has shared her culinary experiences and brilliant recipes with people from all over the world! She plans on expanding into self-help books and dietary cookbooks, so stayed tuned!

Author's Afterthoughts

Thank you for making the decision to invest in one of my cookbooks! I cherish all my readers and hope you find joy in preparing these meals as I have.

There are so many books available and I am truly grateful that you decided to buy this one and follow it from beginning to end.

I love hearing from my readers on what they thought of this book and any value they received from reading it. As a personal favor, I would appreciate any feedback you can give in the form of a review on Amazon and please be honest! This kind of support will help others make an informed choice on and will help me tremendously in producing the best quality books possible.

My most heartfelt thanks,

Nancy Silverman

If you're interested in more of my books, be sure to follow my author page on Amazon (can be found on the link Bellow) or scan the QR-Code.

https://www.amazon.com/author/nancy-silverman

Printed in Great Britain
by Amazon